COOL

SH*T

COOL SH*T

FRANCES READE

weldon**owen**

how to
use this
book

swanky
drinks

slick
moves

dare

wild
pranks

bold
stunts

visual
glossary

index

a note from frances

143 keelhaul a prisoner

Whether your personal icon of awesome is pirate (#143) or rocker (#45), eco-warrior (#80) or card cheat (#2), burlesque babe (#19) or sly prankster (#56), you'll find out how to embody it here. Or if you're just looking for some fun, be it risqué (#86), tasty (#83), mildly dangerous (#53), or just plain stupid (#116), please consider this your guidebook. I've included some activities I would like to see more of in the world, like men wearing ascots (#25) and people riding homemade hoverboards (#103), as well as some activities I'd prefer no one engage in, like drinking pruno (#119). Writing this book, I've drawn on my many daring adventures, from escaping across international borders inside a suitcase (#121) to saving the Earth from an encroaching black hole (#149). Learning to be a better liar (#4)? On my to-do list.

45 give yourself a metal makeover

149 deflect a black hole

FRANCES is a writer and editor who lives in a beautifully decorated (#85) apartment in San Francisco. In her spare time, she enjoys making DIY explosives (#113) with her live-in ninja boyfriend (#142), snuggling with her supervillain pet (#145), and building strange musical instruments (#99). She can hand jive (#37) like nobody's business.

hang fabric wallpaper 85

detonate a dry-ice bomb 113

know your ninja weapons 142

pick your supervillain pet 145

play the electric spatula 99

do the hand jive 37

how to use this book

In the pages that follow, virtually every piece of essential information is presented graphically. In most cases the pictures do, indeed, tell the story. In some cases though, you'll need a little extra information to get it done right. Here's how we present those facts.

CROSS-REFERENCES When one thing just leads to another, we'll point it out. Follow the links for related or interesting information.

sow a seed bomb 80

MATH When measurements matter, find them right in the box. Handy "angle" icons help you do it from the right angle.

½ c (60 g)   90°   2 in (5 cm)

MORE INFORMATION Follow the * symbol to learn more about the how and why of the given step.

ICON GUIDE Throughout the book, handy icons help guide you through critical aspects of time, degree, and more. Here are the icons you'll encounter.

 Check out the timer to learn how much time a relatively short task takes.

 The calendar shows how many days, weeks, or months an activity requires.

 Look to the thermometer to learn the temperature needed for a given action.

 Repeat the depicted action the designated number of times.

 Just how hot, you ask? Cook over low, medium, or high heat, respectively.

A NOTE TO READERS The depictions in this book are presented for entertainment value only. Attempting these activities is not recommended.

- RISKY ACTIVITIES Many of the activities in this book are dangerous. Some are physically impossible. Before attempting any new activity, make sure you are aware of your own limitations and have adequately researched all applicable risks. Good luck with that for #148!

- PROFESSIONAL ADVICE While every item has been carefully researched, this book is not intended to replace professional advice or training of a medical, scientific, culinary, sartorial, romantic, athletic, or martial nature—or any other professional advice, for that matter.

- PHYSICAL AND HEALTH-RELATED ACTIVITIES Be sure to consult a physician before attempting any activity involving physical exertion, particularly if you have a condition that could impair or limit your ability to engage in such an activity, or if you want to avoid looking really silly (for instance, if you try #97).

- ADULT CONTENT The activities in this book are presented solely for the entertainment of adult readers. Please use your common sense and discretion. Not every depiction contains all information necessary to perform a given activity (#151 is harder than it looks, for instance).

- BREAKING THE LAW The information in this book should not be used to break any applicable law or regulation. In other words, just don't even try #15.

impress

1 make loaded dice

Choose your lucky number.

Microwave with your number facing up.

Dice will melt slightly, weighting the bottom.

Bet on your number; rake it in.

2 catch a table talker

"I have a pair."

"I've got two pair."

"I'm holding three of a kind."

"I have a full house."

"Four of a kind, baby!"

Want to squeeze more money from your best friends at poker night? Watch for these classic poker tells and bet accordingly—you'll be bleeding your buddies dry in no time!

If a vein in his forehead is throbbing, maybe he's psyched for a sweet hand.

Chit chatty? A big hand might have him excited.

Is he totally avoiding eye contact? A lame hand might be worrying him.

The sloucher is probably bummed about a weak hand.

You need some answers! Don't get distracted by a pretty face or a pretty story—look for these clues to catch a liar in the act.

When the eyes dart right, the right side of the brain is working on a lie.

If she smiles with her mouth, but not the rest of her face, then she's hiding something.

Liars tend to fidget, especially by touching their hair, neck, or nose.

Even the coolest cucumber will break a sweat during a lie.

A sudden exit betrays discomfort.

Something's amiss when a graceful dame suddenly has a stiff, awkward posture.

Listen for the pitter-patter of (nervously) tapping feet.

Do complex math in your head.

Step on a pin you've stashed in your shoe.

Bite your lip, tongue, or cheek.

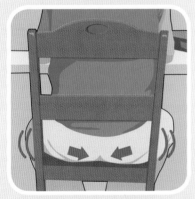

Clench your bottom tightly.

Give one-word answers.

Have your lawyer present.

Got something terrible to hide? During control questions, use these tricks to raise your heart rate and blood pressure. This will give an artificially high baseline reading, so when you lie, your physiological clues might not tip off the tester.

6 — tie a cigarette in a knot

Remove the plastic wrap.

Roll cigarette in wrapper.

Knot the wrapper.

Untie; unwrap.

7 — roll a cigarette one-handed

Set rolling paper fold-down.

Place tobacco on paper.

Pick up, pinching closed.

Roll end-to-end to tamp.

Tuck edge under tobacco.

Roll, tucking entire edge.

Lick; press paper to seal.

Enjoy!

Fill vase with ice water.

Seal the argile to the vase.

Add the tray.

Attach the hose.

Attach the bowl; pack.

Fold hookah foil over; prick.

Place a coal over the bowl.

Brush off ash as it gathers.

set off a smoke screen   114

* Tradition and etiquette dictate that the hookah be placed on the floor during use (you'll probably want to sit down there too for best access). If you're smoking with friends, always hold the hose with your right hand.

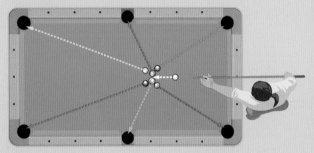

the sneaky pete

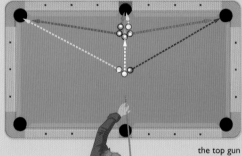

the top gun

132 flee a bar fight unscathed

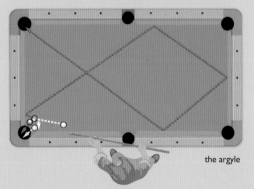

the argyle

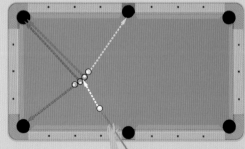

the ugly american

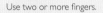

Use two or more fingers.

Toe the line; stand straight.

Hold dart in line with target.

Cock your arm.

Thrust; hold shoulder still.

stun with a poison dart 146

Release with tip slightly up.

Follow through with arm.

Bull's-eye!

While hitting the bull's-eye is the most visually impressive feat in darts, hitting 17–20 in the triple ring will earn you more points.

double ring (double points)

triple ring (triple points)

bull (25 points)

bull's-eye (50 points)

3 fl oz (90 ml) gin

1 tbsp vermouth

1

2

3

4

Shaken or stirred? Those who like it a little rough go with shaking—it adds a little water and slivers of ice for an edgy chill. Smooth types prefer stirred martinis for their silky, refined texture.

naked
3 fl oz (90 ml) gin
1 green olive garnish

gibson
3 fl oz (90 ml) gin
1 tbsp dry vermouth
1 pearl onion garnish

cooperstown
3 tbsp gin
1 tbsp sweet vermouth
1 tbsp dry vermouth
1 mint sprig garnish

cosmo
2 fl oz (60 ml) citrus vodka
1 tbsp triple sec
1 tbsp cranberry juice
1 tbsp lime juice
1 lime wedge garnish

vesper
1¼ fl oz (35 ml) gin
1¼ fl oz (35 ml) vodka
1 tbsp Lillet Blanc
1 lemon wedge garnish

cajun
2½ fl oz (75 ml)
pepper vodka
1 tbsp dry vermouth
1 jalapeño pepper garnish

bacontini
3 fl oz (90 ml) vodka
1 dash vermouth
1 bacon strip garnish

saketini
2½ fl oz (75 ml) gin
1½ tsp sake
1 green olive garnish

tequilatini
2½ fl oz (75 ml) tequila
1½ tsp sweet vermouth
1 maraschino cherry garnish

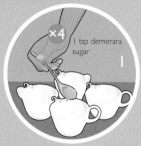

×4

1 tsp demerara sugar

I

Add lemon twists and sugar.

4 fl oz (120 ml) boiling water

2

Pour boiling water into mug.

8

Fill cups. Extinguish before drinking!

5 fl oz (150 ml) single malt scotch

3

Quickly add scotch.

×4

7

Repeat, wearing a blasé expression.

6

Pour back, from a greater height.

5

Pour three-quarters into second mug.

4

Light with a long match.

3 fl oz (90 ml) absinthe

1 lump sugar

Put on an absinthe spoon.

4–6 fl oz (120–180 ml) ice water

Dilute to taste.

*

In this Czech variation on a French theme, the sugar cube is dipped in absinthe and set ablaze. (Don't get too carried away—absinthe's high alcohol content makes it very flammable.) After the sugar melts, dilute the drink, then serve it promptly to the nearest wild-eyed bohemian. Na zdraví!

This is a dangerous process, and doing it wrong can result in blindness or death, so be sure you consult a qualified chemist or hillbilly.

1 Combine all-corn hog feed and water in a still. Use pure cornmeal hog feed with no fillers, such as sawdust.

2 Light coals; bring the liquid to a boil.

3 Add sugar and yeast to boiling liquid.

56 perform a pig prank

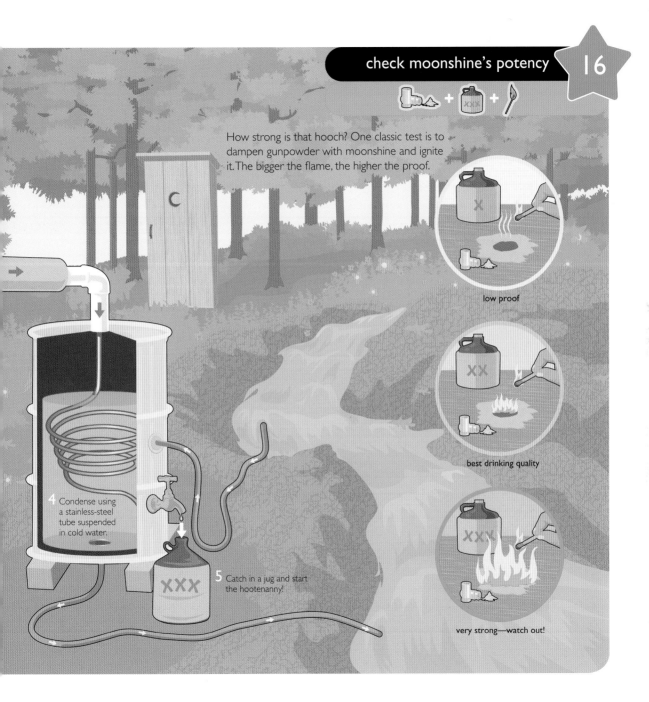

How strong is that hooch? One classic test is to dampen gunpowder with moonshine and ignite it. The bigger the flame, the higher the proof.

low proof

best drinking quality

very strong—watch out!

4 Condense using a stainless-steel tube suspended in cold water.

5 Catch in a jug and start the hootenanny!

17 dance the charleston

Step back onto right foot.

Kick left leg to side.

Step forward onto left foot.

Kick right leg to side.

18 infuse your booze

½ c (50 g) fresh ginger

Grate fresh ginger.

Add to a mason jar.

24 fl oz (750 ml) vodka

Cover with vodka; seal jar.

Store in a cool, dark place.

Shake once a day.

Pour through a sieve; serve.

Plain liquor can be infused with just about any flavor—instead of ginger try fruit, herbs, or even cooked bacon.

19   do a burlesque glove peel

Stroke your gloved arm.

Saucily bite index fingertip.

Pull each tip to loosen glove.

Pull it off, twirl overhead.

20   kick up the can can

Hold skirt above your knees.

Lift right toe to left knee.

Step back with right foot.

Kick to reveal thighs.

Lift left toe to right knee.

Step back with left foot.

Kick.

Display derriere.

craft personalized pasties 21

Draw areola-size circles.

Cut out the circles.

Cut line; glue into cones.

Personalize your pasties.

Poke a hole in cone's point.

Thread in the tassel; knot.

Trim excess thread.

Affix to skin with spirit gum.

twirl your tassels 22

Bend knees; bounce.

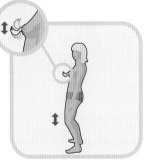

Bounce more vigorously.

shimmy up walls 136

Lean to set tassels a-twirl.

Lift arm to change direction.

23   fashion a fabulous fingerwave

Put setting lotion in wet hair.

Wiggle to make waves.

Set waves with fingers.

24   tease up a bouffant

Create four sections; clip.

Curl each section.

Spray heavily with hair spray.

Tease from bottom to top.

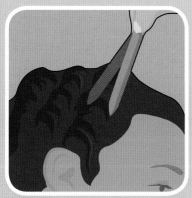

Secure with clips as you go.

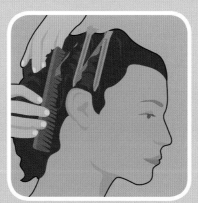

Continue until complete.

Remove clips.

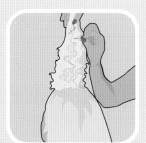

Pin the sections; continue.

Smooth with paddle brush.

Shape a curl in front.

Spray more hair spray.

Drape ascot around neck.

Loop right end under left.

Cross right end back over.

Slide up inside neck knot.

Bring right end down.

Adjust to cover knot.

Tuck into shirt.

Fluff it out. Dandy!

26 identify men's furnishings

tie clip

stick pin

cuff links

watch with fob

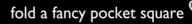

Fold handkerchief in half.

Crease top layer at point.

Fold corner made by crease.

Crease and fold next corner.

Crease and fold next corner.

Fold bottom under.

Fold right side under.

Place in jacket pocket.

Remove dirt with a brush.

Apply polish. Let dry.

Brush again.

Buff to a high shine.

29 face the world as a flapper

Pluck or pencil a thin, high arch.

Rim eye in dark pencil; smudge.

Pat skin with rice powder.

Draw a heart-shaped pout; fill.

30 conquer with ww2 makeup

Lengthen and darken brows with a pencil.

Sweep on subtle eyeshadow.

Start with a dark foundation; apply light powder.

Exaggerate top lip; use bold lipstick.

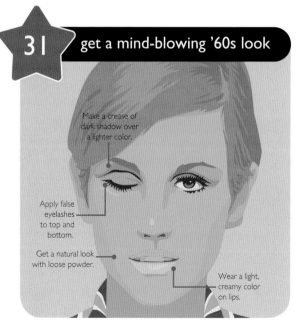

31 get a mind-blowing '60s look

Make a crease of dark shadow over a lighter color.

Apply false eyelashes to top and bottom.

Get a natural look with loose powder.

Wear a light, creamy color on lips.

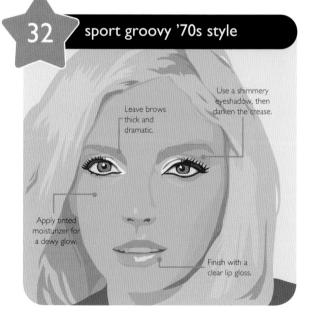

32 sport groovy '70s style

Leave brows thick and dramatic.

Use a shimmery eyeshadow, then darken the crease.

Apply tinted moisturizer for a dewy glow.

Finish with a clear lip gloss.

apply and remove false lashes ⭐33

come out as a drag queen 90

Trim to length of your eye.

Apply glue to the back.

Place along the lash line.

Hold in place as it dries.

Curl fake and real lashes.

Apply mascara.

Petroleum jelly will un-glue.

Gently pull loose to remove.

draw on dramatic eyes ⭐34

Warm eye pencil briefly.

Blow on pencil to set.

Apply lavishly.

Rock like an Egyptian.

35 style an authentic ducktail

Apply pomade liberally.

Part hair in back.

Comb sides straight back.

Fold ends into back part.

 Wear the jeans for a week or two, so they'll continue molding to your form. Then it's time to jump in the tub again. Repeat this process until your pants are suitably tight.

36 get perfectly shrunk jeans

Fill tub with hot water.

Get in, wearing your jeans.

Stay in tub until water cools.

Air-dry without removing.

Pat thighs.

Clap.

Pass one hand above other.

Switch.

Tap one fist onto other.

Switch.

Point thumb over shoulder.

Point with other thumb.

carry smokes in a sleeve 38

Stash one for later.

Lay sideways above hem.

Pull hem over pack, pinch.

Roll pack over into sleeve.

"get on up" from a split

Stretch your legs.

Leap with hips facing right.

Slide down into a split.

Land it.

Push with hand; bend leg.

Drag your heel to stand.

Put foot behind knee.

Put ball of foot on ground.

Open your right thigh; spin.

Raise up as you turn.

End facing front.

Fall to knees in celebration.

41 pull a tablecloth off a set table

 + + +

Place the cloth at the edge.

Smooth any wrinkles.

Add heavy items.

42 bring a dove back to life

Craft a dummy head.

Conceal the dummy.

Choose a mark.

Tuck dove's head; hold fake.

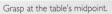
Grasp at the table's midpoint.

Pull downward briskly.

Admire your handiwork.

Simulate decapitation.

Cover the dove.

Blow to raise dove's head.

Release; hiding dummy.

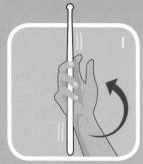

Hold a drumstick loosely.

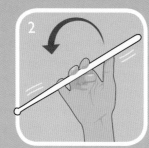

Roll it over middle finger.

Let it roll upright.

Roll it over ring finger.

Catch and roll over pinkie.

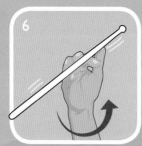

Roll to index finger; repeat.

spin a guitar 44

Lock the strap; hold at waist.

Step over the cord.

Push guitar base up, over.

Swing it upright; rock out.

give yourself a metal makeover 45

Apply base to face and neck.

Set with powder.

Draw bat shapes in liner.

Line eyelids.

Fill the shapes with shadow.

Line lips.

Fill lips with dark lipstick.

Brutal.

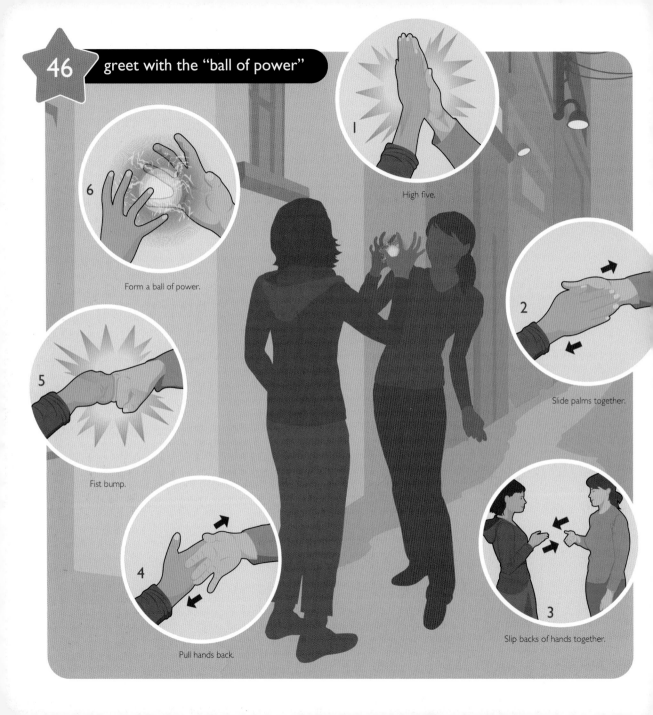

1. High five.

6. Form a ball of power.

2. Slide palms together.

5. Fist bump.

4. Pull hands back.

3. Slip backs of hands together.

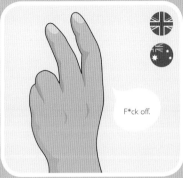

the v-sign

the bird

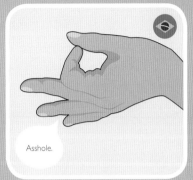

the ring

the hook

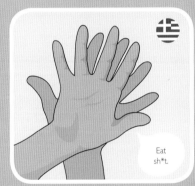

moutza

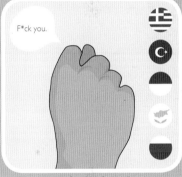

mano fico (the fig hand)

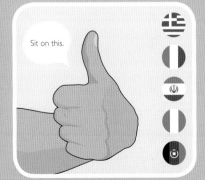

thumbs up

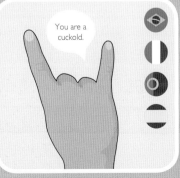

mano cornuta (the horns)

concha (the shell)

48 execute a high kick

Crouch.

Step onto left foot.

Swing right leg forward.

Leap off left foot.

49 fight with nunchakus

Hold over shoulder.

Grip close to joint.

Bend wrist to begin rotation.

Flick wrist forward.

Kick left foot as right falls.

Land on right foot.

Plant left foot.

Catch balance.

Thrust arm down to side.

Pull arm back to shoulder.

Strike across chest to hip.

Cross hips; return to start.

Continue this basic flicking motion as you execute the arm moves. Tip: Real ninjas never hit themselves in the face!

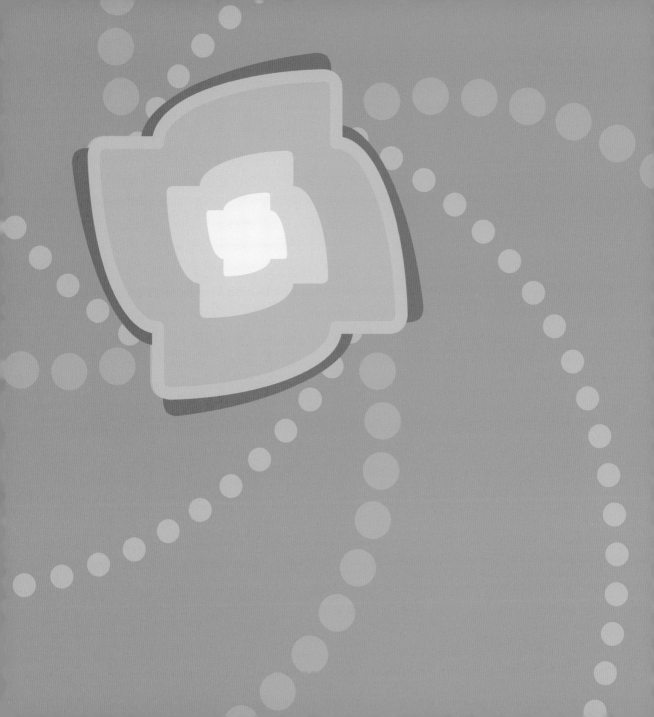

amuse

Grip near end of handle.

Raise mallet overhead.

Arch back slightly.

Take a few test swings.

Hit right in target's center.

Gloat.

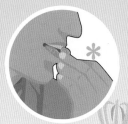
Secretly lick coin.

Lean in as far as possible.

Throw in a high arc.

COIN TOSS

Camies will put a slick coating on the plates. Foil them by wetting your coin to make it stickier.

ace the balloon darts 52

Aim at a balloon near edge.

Throw dart in a high curve.

The balloons are extra-thick; hit one repeatedly.

turn a pen into a crossbow

Dismantle a pen.

Drill hole halfway up barrel.

Push the pen tip through.

Cut two notches at ends.

Attach a pencil.

Put rubber band in notches.

Tape down a clothespin.

Clip inkwell into clothespin.

✳ It's all fun and games until someone loses an eye.
Don't aim this at people—it's pointy!

Take pen apart; drill hole.

Insert pen barrel into hole.

Drill a hole in the bottom.

Make a spitball.

Load spitball into barrel.

Pour rubbing alcohol.

2 tsp rubbing alcohol

Plug hole; shake vigorously.

Aim; hold match to hole.

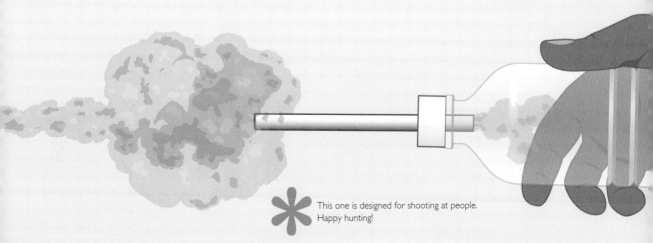

* This one is designed for shooting at people. Happy hunting!

make crop circles

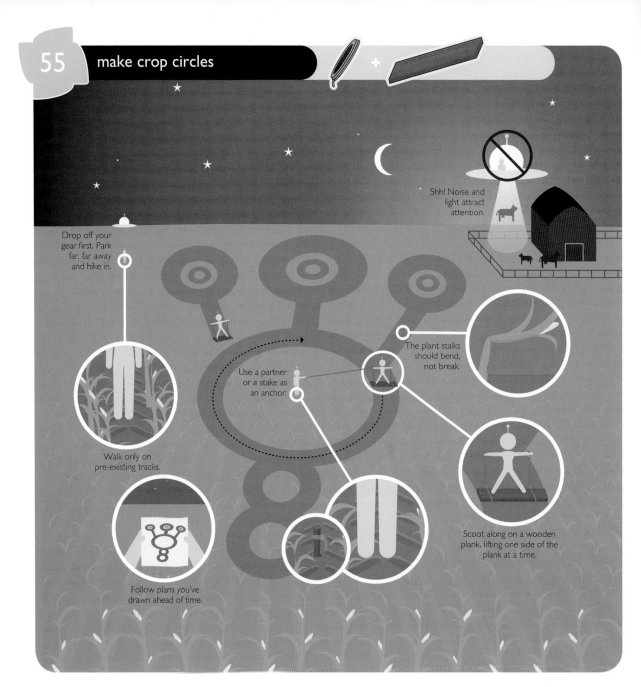

Drop off your gear first. Park far, far away and hike in.

Shh! Noise and light attract attention.

Use a partner or a stake as an anchor.

The plant stalks should bend, not break.

Walk only on pre-existing tracks.

Scoot along on a wooden plank, lifting one side of the plank at a time.

Follow plans you've drawn ahead of time.

 +

Grease three pigs.

Mark them "1," "2," and "4."

Set loose in a public area.

Watch them search for "3."

Fill the vents with confetti, then turn the heat on high so that the confetti erupts on ignition.

Squirt toothpaste under the door handles for a sticky surprise.

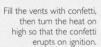
Put salami slices on the windshield for enduring grease spots.

Put a condom on the tailpipe. It'll inflate impressively.

For a lingering stench, place a dead fish on the air intake.

Roll down the window, then sprinkle broken safety glass on the ground.

2 Season a salmon fillet over tinfoil.

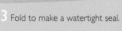

3 Fold to make a watertight seal.

4 Place on top rack.

5 Run full cycle, including drying.

Drive; feel for hottest point.

Shape foil into hollow cone.

Set on hot spot; close hood.

Remove foil; gauge space.

Wrap food in layers of foil.

Place securely on manifold.

Close hood; drive.

Unwrap; test for doneness.

The cone will show you how much space is available between the manifold and the hood. Pick a food item that will fit snugly without getting smashed. If you have too much space, pad the food with little balls of foil.

time a tasty trip | 60

chicken drumstick
2–3 hours

shrimp
30–45 minutes

pork tenderloin
4 hours

chicken breast
45–60 minutes

salmon or trout
60–90 minutes

61 bunny-hop a bike

1 Crouch low.

2 Hop up, pulling the handlebars.

3 Keep pulling. Point your toes down.

4 Tuck your legs up to raise the back wheel.

5 Land it!

1 Pedal forward.

2 Push one pedal down hard and jerk backward.

3 Lean back farther and pull up on the handlebars.

4 Keep your balance.

5 Lean forward, pushing down on the handlebars.

6 Keep riding.

63 paint an art car

Coat exposed strips with metal enamel.

Once dry, stencil on designs.

Add details by hand.

Tape newspaper strips at regular intervals.

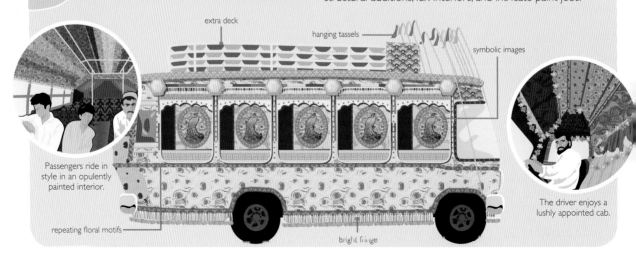

64 ponder pakistani bus art

Art buses are big business in Pakistan—bus owners pay craftsmen thousands of dollars to pimp their rides with structural additions, lux interiors, and intricate paint jobs.

extra deck

hanging tassels

symbolic images

Passengers ride in style in an opulently painted interior.

The driver enjoys a lushly appointed cab.

repeating floral motifs

bright fringe

Collect kitschy items according to theme.

Glue pieces to car with liquid silicon.

Attach ceramic tiles with art epoxy.

Paint over finished work with sealant.

A subculture that started with fishing transport trucks in northeastern Japan, dekotora has been popularized since the 1970s in movies, anime, and video games.

chrome omamentation

fantastical airbrushed scenes

The living quarters inside are as blinging as the exterior.

A chandelier lights the driver's way.

hundreds of lights flashing in sequence

build a bike ramp

3

Screw the side pieces
onto the rear frame.

4

Slip joist planks
between the sides
and screw in.

5

Attach the ramp
face in two layers.

2

Assemble six planks
for the rear frame.

1

Cut out the curved
side pieces.

slide into a whipskid **68**

Track bikes are indoor racing bikes with one gear and no hand brakes. Today "fixies" are beloved by urban daredevils and show-offs. Try these fixie tricks at your own risk.

Move weight forward.

Lower center of gravity.

Lock knees to stop wheels.

do a smoky burnout **128**

Skid; use your hips to fishtail.

trackstand with no hands **69**

Stand with feet parallel.

Turn front wheel slightly.

Shift feet to balance.

Remove hands; sit upright.

6 Grab the toe edge between your feet.

7 Let go before you land.

1 Put one foot at the board's center and one foot at its tail.

2 Kick the tail down. Drag your front foot up the board.

3 Lift both knees to your chest while clearing the steps.

4 Land and shred away.

5 Ollie as high as you can, bending knees.

4 Crouch down as you ascend the wall.

1 Dive into a handstand; grab board over trucks.

2 Bend your knees. Jerk the board up.

3 Flick the board. Pull knees up to chest.

4 Land with both feet over the trucks.

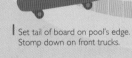

1 Set tail of board on pool's edge. Stomp down on front trucks.

2 Lean forward to gather momentum.

3 Skate on, brah.

1. Insert a funnel into a tube.

2. Secure tube with a clamp.

3. Insert a valve into free end.

4. Imbibe at amazing speeds!

Tilt can to form air pocket.

Jab hole in air pocket.

Lean; put mouth over hole.

Tilt up, opening tab. Chug.

Grab the rim; lift a leg.

Kick up your other leg.

Drink from the nozzle.

Shake leg when finished.

2 c (475 ml) boiling water

1 packet dessert gelatin

Combine; stir to dissolve.

Cool to room temperature.

2 c (400 ml) chilled vodka

Stir in chilled vodka.

Coat with cooking spray.

Add little spoons.

infuse your booze 18

Pour gelatin mix.

6 hrs

Refrigerate.

Shoot or scoop out.

Core the apple halfway.

Take apart pen; keep barrel.

Plug with finger; light; inhale.

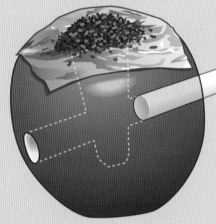

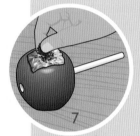

Pack bowl.

Force barrel through apple.

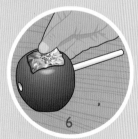

Place foil over hole.

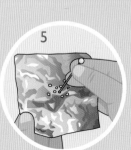

Poke holes in a bit of foil.

Clear barrel; reinsert.

Cut bottom off plastic jug.

Make a hole in the cap.

Make a foil bowl over hole.

Poke holes in the foil.

Place in bucket of water.

Pack; screw cap on.

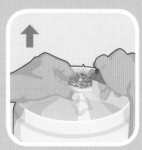

Light; pull bottle up.

inhale your morning coffee 120

Uncap; push down; inhale.

Apply glue to pages' edges.

Insert cardboard; let dry.

Cut out the interior; glue.

Fill with guilty pleasures.

sow a seed bomb

½ c (70 g) seeds

¾ c (200 g) compost

1

Pour seeds over compost.

1⅓ c (350 g) red clay

2

Mix in clay.

Guerilla gardening is a homegrown movement aiming to make public spaces greener and prettier. Here are two quick ways to reclaim your cityscape.

1 c (240 ml) water

3

Stir in water.

4

Roll marble-size "bombs."

5

Dry in the sun.

6

Launch before a rain.

Pick a hardy plant that won't require much care, and that is indigenous to your area.

handful of moss

2 c (500 ml) beer

Pour beer; crumble moss.

½ tsp sugar

2 c (475 ml) buttermilk

Add sugar and buttermilk.

Blend until frothy.

Paint onto wood or brick.

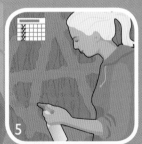

Mist weekly.

Watch your art grow.

infuse tasty truffles

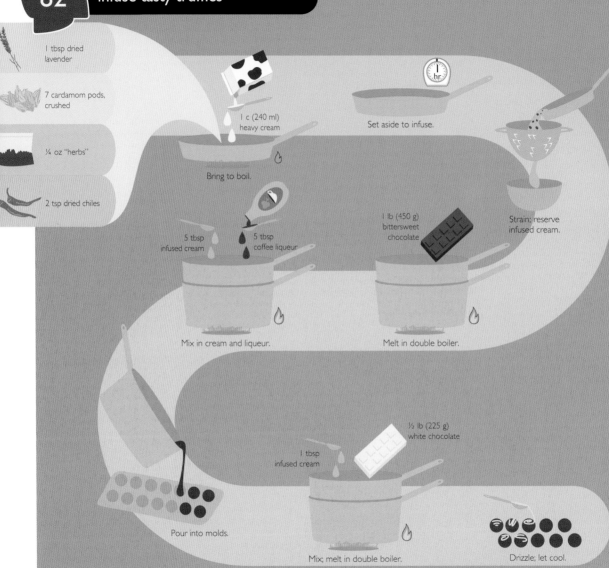

1 tbsp dried lavender

7 cardamom pods, crushed

¼ oz "herbs"

2 tsp dried chiles

1 c (240 ml) heavy cream

Bring to boil.

Set aside to infuse.

Strain; reserve infused cream.

5 tbsp infused cream

5 tbsp coffee liqueur

Mix in cream and liqueur.

1 lb (450 g) bittersweet chocolate

Melt in double boiler.

Pour into molds.

1 tbsp infused cream

½ lb (225 g) white chocolate

Mix; melt in double boiler.

Drizzle; let cool.

2 peaches

Slice peaches lengthwise.

3 tbsp butter

Melt in an enamel pan.

2 tbsp brown sugar

Stir in brown sugar.

Add fruit; cook until soft.

Flip peaches over.

¼ c (60 ml) rum

Pour rum over peaches.

Ignite with a kitchen match.

Serve over ice cream.

84 create hipster decoupage

Clean intended surface.

Cut out pop-culture images.

Arrange cut-outs.

Glue cut-outs.

85 hang fabric wallpaper

Wash the wall.

Measure the wall.

2 in (5 cm)

2 in (5 cm)

Measure; add overhang; cut.

Pour liquid starch in a pan.

When you're ready for a decor makeover, just peel the
fabric off the wall—it won't leave residue or harm the paint.

Smooth as you go.

Once dry, layer varnish.

Let dry; sand down.

Repeat until smooth.

Brush starch up wall.

Stick on, leaving overhang.

Cover wall and let dry.

Trim off excess fabric.

Tear out a picture.

Outline in black marker.

Tape to a bright window.

Tape fabric over page.

Trace on fabric with pencil.

Remove.

Place in embroidery hoop.

Stitch with embroidery floss.

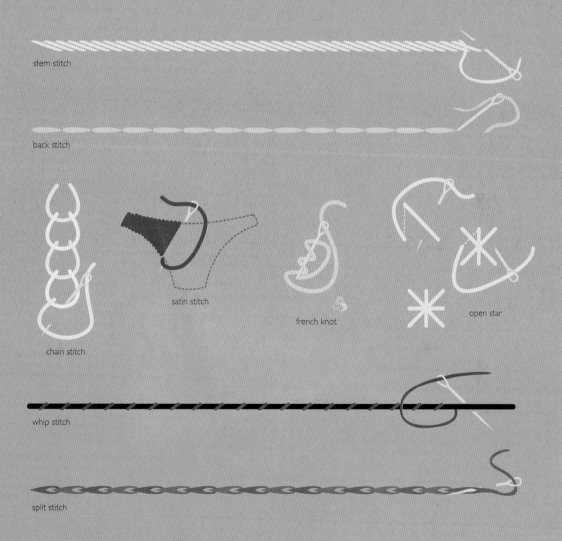

stem stitch

back stitch

chain stitch

satin stitch

french knot

open star

whip stitch

split stitch

Cut top off a large bottle.

Shave area to be cast.

Pour; tap to release bubbles.

Prepare plaster.

1 c (120 g) alginate
¼ c (60 ml) water

Knead bag to mix.

Pull from container slowly.

Pour into the bottle.

5–10 min

Thrust in body part; let set.

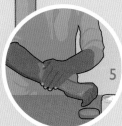
Coat area in petroleum jelly.

Worried about getting a sensitive body part stuck while casting? Don't be—alginate forms a flexible, rubbery mold.

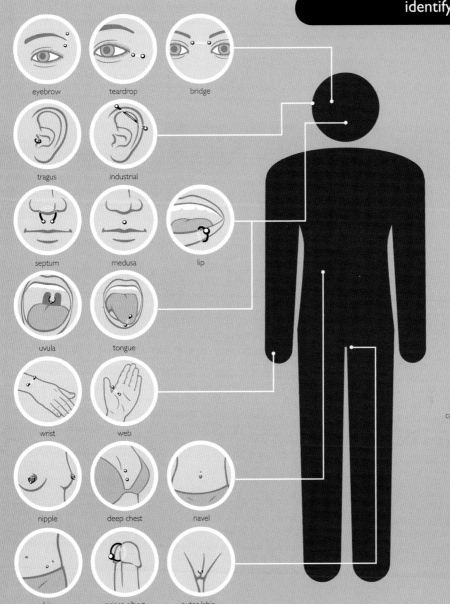

eyebrow

teardrop

bridge

tragus

industrial

septum

medusa

lip

uvula

tongue

wrist

web

nipple

deep chest

navel

hip

prince albert

outer labia

flesh tunnel

plug

claw

crescent

open spiral

open ring

captive bead ring

barbell

curved barbell

prince's wand

Fill a full-coverage bra with pillow stuffing.

Diamonds are a girl's best friend—they cover up her Adam's apple.

A wig cap keeps stray hairs under control.

135 hide valuables securely

Tight, high-cut undies hide unsightly bulges.

Spackle face and chest with foundation.

No one will see your man hands and hairy arms beneath elegant opera gloves!

A corset helps give that womanly figure.

Three layers of sheer stockings a shade darker than your skin will hide any muscles.

Go glam with the makeup.

Cut hair long on top, short on the sides.

A suit with padded shoulders adds bulk.

Bind chest with wide bandages.

Cut sideburns at a square angle.

Imagine your center of gravity is near your sternum, and adjust your stance accordingly.

When you walk, lead with your crotch. For increased realism, let your crotch lead your behavior as well!

An undershirt helps conceal curves.

Dab burnt cork on lightly for five o'clock shadow.

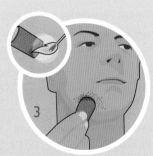

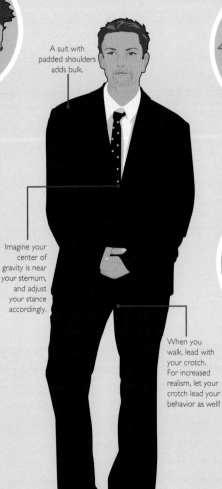

Roll and place a sock for enhanced manliness.

92 shave with a straight razor

Start with a hot shower.

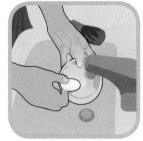

Set soap cake in hot water.

Mix into lather.

144 light your pirate beard on fire

Cover beard in lather.

×50

Strop to sharpen.

Pull skin, shave with grain.

Re-lather, mow against grain.

Rinse with cold water.

93 chrome your dome

Apply shaving cream; shave.

107 be a human cannonball

Exfoliate.

Towel dry.

Rub on aloe vera.

spike a mohawk 94

Backcomb.

Apply glue generously.

Blow-dry against a surface.

Spray to hold.

flaunt a fauxhawk 95

Wash, then dry hair.

Gel hair up and forward.

Hold with hair spray.

Enjoy your awesomeness.

identify men's facial hair styles 96

freestyle

wolverine

bishop

french fork

napoleon III imperial

imperial

Prepare to stand on head.

Kick your legs up.

Open your legs.

Twist hips for momentum.

Snap hips to face front.

Pull hands off ground; spin.

40 rock a dynamite stage spin

Slow; return hands to floor.

Swing legs clockwise.

3 Move the fader to the center; play the sample.

2 Select a sample.

4 Return the fader to the left; playing only the main track.

1 With the fader to the left, play the main track.

5 Rewind the sample.

6 Move the fader to the center; play the sample again.

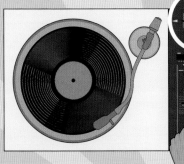

play the electric spatula

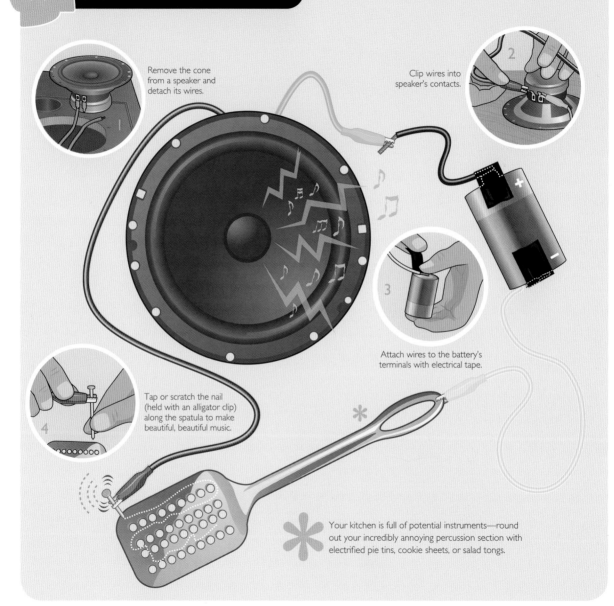

Remove the cone from a speaker and detach its wires.

Clip wires into speaker's contacts.

Attach wires to the battery's terminals with electrical tape.

Tap or scratch the nail (held with an alligator clip) along the spatula to make beautiful, beautiful music.

✳ Your kitchen is full of potential instruments—round out your incredibly annoying percussion section with electrified pie tins, cookie sheets, or salad tongs.

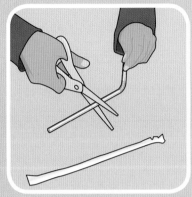

Cut a straw in half; discard the bendy part.

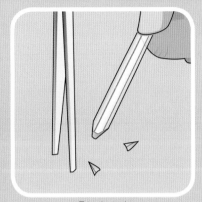

Trim the end.

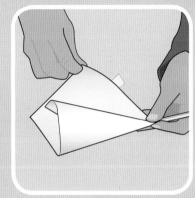

Tape paper into a cone around the straw.

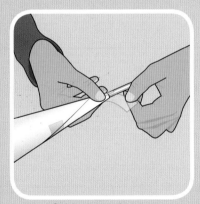

Seal the paper to the straw.

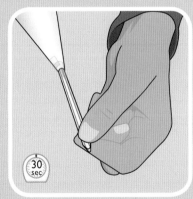

Pinch the end tightly.

Honk until someone takes it away.

create speaker monsters

 + +

½ c (60 g) cornstarch
1 c (240 ml) water

Mix cornstarch and water.

Pour onto a baking tray.

Upturn a speaker and
wrap in plastic.

Set the pan on the speaker;
kick out the jams.

 Dear God, is it alive? Nope, it's just
a simple non-Newtonian fluid,
demonstrating the properties of
both a solid and a liquid.

 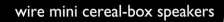

Unfold, flatten two boxes.

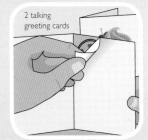

2 talking greeting cards

Peel open the cards.

×2

Remove the speakers.

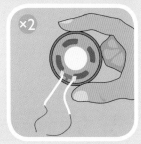

×2

Cut wires at circuit board.

Cut off two earbuds.

Strip; cut away any fibers.

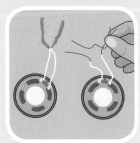

Twist wires together; tape.

Trace speaker; cut out.

Cut a notch at the bottom.

Glue in speakers.

Run wires out notches; glue.

Plug in and rock out.

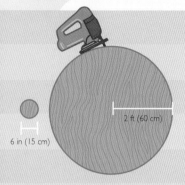

6 in (15 cm)

2 ft (60 cm)

1 Cut two discs from plywood.

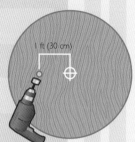

1 ft (30 cm)

2 Cut a hole the size of a leaf-blower nozzle.

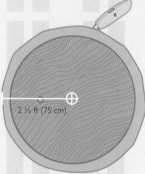

2 ½ ft (75 cm)

3 Cut a circle from a plastic tarp.

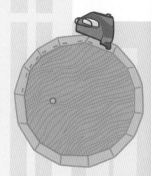

4 Center large wood disc over tarp; staple down.

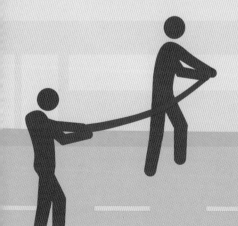

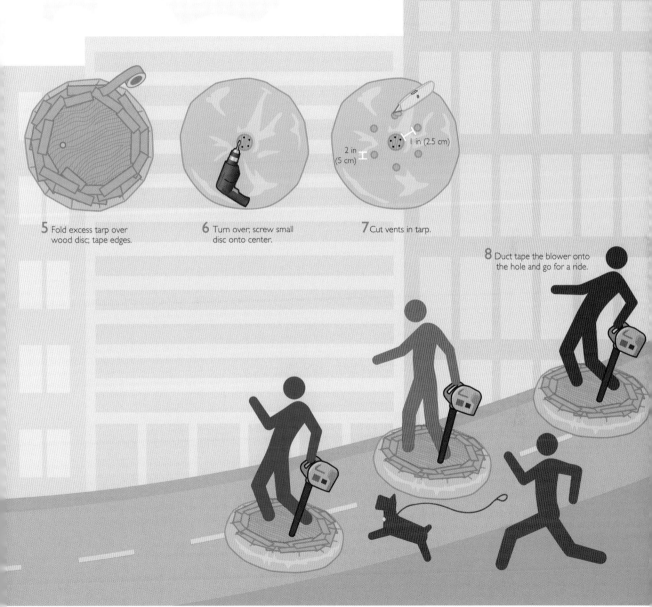

5 Fold excess tarp over wood disc; tape edges.

6 Turn over; screw small disc onto center.

7 Cut vents in tarp.

2 in (5 cm)

1 in (2.5 cm)

8 Duct tape the blower onto the hole and go for a ride.

dare

104 jump out of an airplane

1 Leap from the plane.

13,000 ft
(4 km)

2 Enjoy your free fall!

3 Pull out the pilot chute.

2,500 ft
(750 m)

105 descend in style

head-down ring

solo skysurfing

tandem

star

4 The pilot chute catches air . . .

2,200 ft
(650 m)

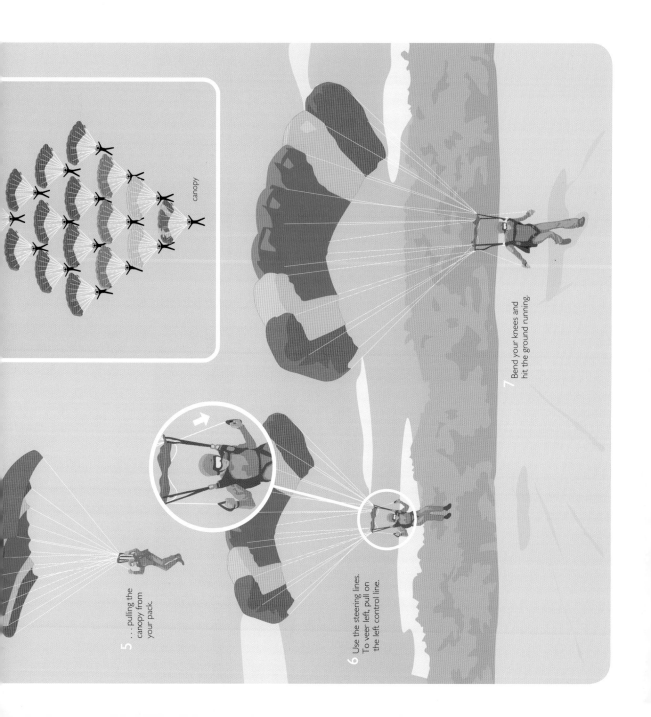

5 . . . pulling the canopy from your pack

canopy

6 Use the steering lines. To veer left, pull on the left control line.

7 Bend your knees and hit the ground running.

travel by jet pack

1

Strap in securely.

2

Pull throttle to take off.

3

Push bars to go forward.

4

Steer with left hand.

5

Push throttle down to land.

6

Happy landing!

Climb inside the cannon.

Lie down in hydraulic-powered canister.

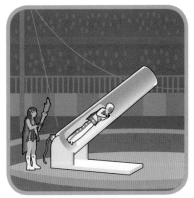

Ignite firecrackers for a big bang.

Activate hydraulic canister.

Tuck body to flip.

Land on net.

All the smoke and fire (and the caped assistant) are just for show. The daredevil is "shot" by a hydraulic-powered canister—no singed jumpsuits here!

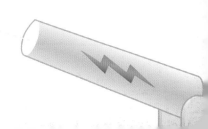

kite surf the open ocean

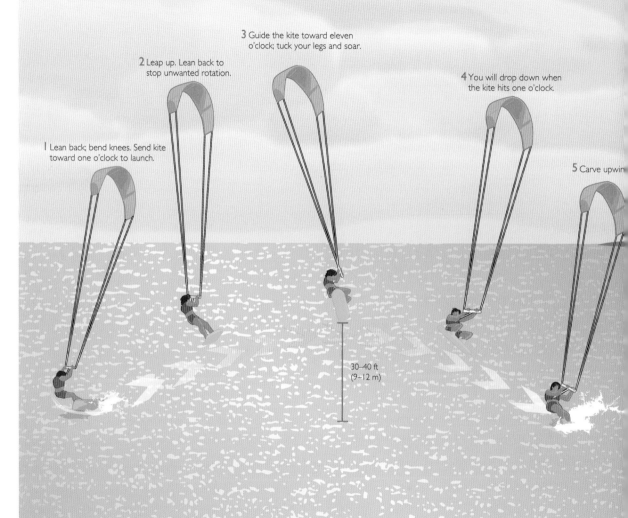

1 Lean back; bend knees. Send kite toward one o'clock to launch.

2 Leap up. Lean back to stop unwanted rotation.

3 Guide the kite toward eleven o'clock; tuck your legs and soar.

4 You will drop down when the kite hits one o'clock.

5 Carve upwin

30–40 ft
(9–12 m)

A ridge lift is created when the wind hits an obstacle (like a cliff) and is diverted sharply upward. Hang gliders zigzag up the wind column to gain serious altitude.

4 Spot 50–200 ft (15–60 m) of clear space to land on.

3 When you hit the ridge lift, crisscross to climb.

1 Strap into glider. Run off cliff.

2 Steer by shifting your weight to change the glider's center of gravity.

5 Point the glider up as you near the ground, and glide into the wind.

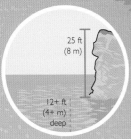

25 ft (8 m)

12+ ft (4+ m) deep

Find a safe jumping site.

Check for rocks.

Stand as straight as possible.

Jump!

Keep safety supplies nearby.

Light; check the wind.

Milk neutralizes kerosene.

1 tsp kerosene

Hold in your mouth.

6 in
(15 cm)

Spray a mist of kerosene.

Move the torch down.

Wipe with a damp rag.

Bread soaks up the fuel.

Drill a hole through a pipe.

2 ft (60 cm) steel pipe

Insert chain.

12 ft (4 m) metal chain

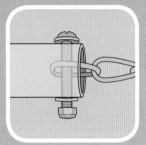

Secure with nuts and bolt.

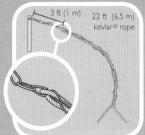

Weave rope toward end.

3 ft (1 m)   22 ft (6.5 m) kevlar® rope

Tie at the bottom.

Coil chain; dip in kerosene.

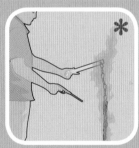

Hold away from body; light.

*

Snuff with wet towel.

* Fire whips are impressive; a trip to the hospital isn't.
Always have a bucket of water with a towel in it
and a fire extinguisher handy.

113 detonate a dry-ice bomb

Break dry ice into chunks.

Fill one quarter of bottle.

water at room temperature

Fill two-thirds of bottle.

Cap bottle.

Throw immediately.

sow a seed bomb 80

Await explosion.

If it doesn't blow right away, for goodness' sake don't go near it. These can take up to fifteen minutes to explode.

Grind into a fine powder.

½ c (60 g) stump remover

Mix over very low heat.

3 tbsp sugar

ground stump remover

Cook into a brown paste.

10–15 min

Spoon into cardboard tube.

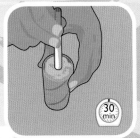

Stick pen in center; let dry.

30 min

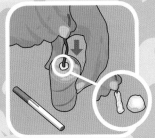

Insert fuse packed in cotton.

Duct tape entire tube.

Light outside; move back.

The active ingredient in this smoke bomb is potassium nitrate, which is found in stump remover. It's also sold as saltpeter, niter, and E252.

Want to instantly communicate something to everyone you meet for the rest of your life? Try a tattoo! These coded symbols are drawn from prison, tribal, and naval traditions.

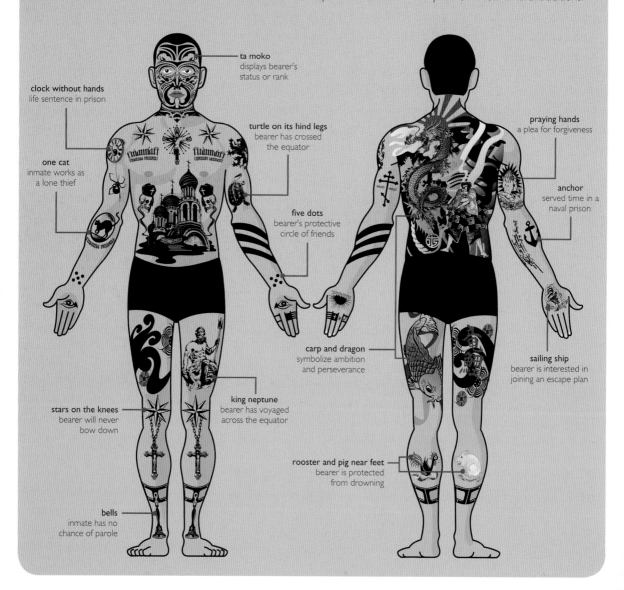

clock without hands
life sentence in prison

one cat
inmate works as
a lone thief

ta moko
displays bearer's
status or rank

turtle on its hind legs
bearer has crossed
the equator

five dots
bearer's protective
circle of friends

praying hands
a plea for forgiveness

anchor
served time in a
naval prison

stars on the knees
bearer will never
bow down

king neptune
bearer has voyaged
across the equator

carp and dragon
symbolize ambition
and perseverance

sailing ship
bearer is interested in
joining an escape plan

bells
inmate has no
chance of parole

rooster and pig near feet
bearer is protected
from drowning

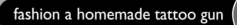
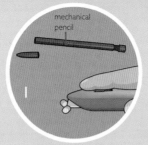

mechanical pencil

Remove the tip and eraser; cut the eraser in half.

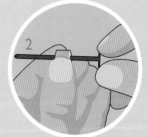

Poke a hole in one eraser half; discard the other.

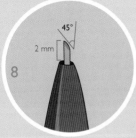

45°
2 mm

Cut wire at angle just above pencil tip.

7

Tape the pencil tip onto brush.

9 Dip the tip into a bottle of ink; practice—a lot—on a banana peel before trying on a human.

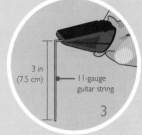

3 in (7.5 cm) | 11-gauge guitar string

3

Cut guitar string; bend the tip into a right angle.

6

Push firmly onto metal shaft.

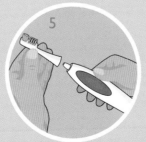

5

Remove tip of toothbrush.

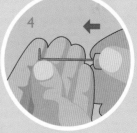

4

Slide the wire through the eraser half.

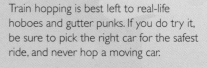

Train hopping is best left to real-life hoboes and gutter punks. If you do try it, be sure to pick the right car for the safest ride, and never hop a moving car.

Sneak past the guard.

Ask worker for departures.

Watch out for rolling cars.

Enter stationary, open car.

Jam door; enjoy the ride.

Exit when train slows.

out-of-service car

tank car

full gondola car

empty gondola car

Hollow out, saving top.

Prepare the cake batter.

Fill halfway with batter; top.

Wrap each in foil.

Place in coals; turn often.

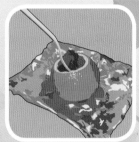

Unwrap and serve.

empty boxcar

119   ferment a vile brew

1 can fruit in syrup
12 oranges

Place in trash bag.

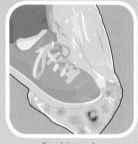

Smash into pulp.

2 c (475 ml) hot water

Add water; shake well.

Seal with rubber bands; wait.

120   inhale your morning coffee

¾ lb (340 g) coffee beans

Grind coffee.

3 min

2 c (475 ml) water

Boil in water.

Strain; discard grounds.

15 min

Boil into a syrup.

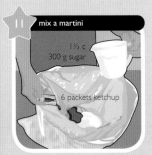

1½ c
300 g sugar

6 packets ketchup

Add sugar and ketchup.

Squeeze to blend.

Release gas once daily.

Strain; drink at own risk.

This revolting liquor is popular in prisons and boot camps.
(Americans know it as "pruno.") There is no reason for
a free man to make or consume this beverage.

2 tbsp
plain
ammonia

Add plain ammonia.

Cook into tar, stirring often.

Scrape tar into pipe.

Light; become very awake.

Careful, some types of ammonia have dangerous additives.
To be on the safe side, never, ever do this.

abscond in a suitcase

Cut large notches in ends of suitcases.

Cover the holes with stickers.

Arrange a distraction; sneak on the train.

Set up with the holes facing each other.

Climb up and close yourself in.

Stay quiet during the ride.

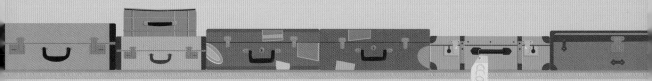

Fold stronger arm in; inhale.

Exhale, making wiggle room.

Hang upside down.

Remove jacket with flair.

Hook the sleeve belt; pull.

Holding your dominant arm against your body makes it easier to push your elbow over your head later.

Wiggle your elbows.

Undo back belts.

Bite to undo the sleeve belt.

Uncross and raise arms.

Push elbow toward head.

Use multiple anchors.

Tie into your harness.

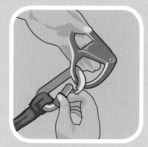

Clip on the rappel device.

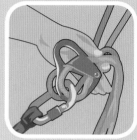

Thread in two ropes; close.

4 in (10 cm)

Grasp the rope.

Grab the excess.

Wind around hip.

Walk down cliff face.

climbing shoes

webbing; carabiners

rappel device; rope

chalk bag

harness

build a hoverboard 103

1. Roll down window.

2. Open door when possible. *

3. Undo seat belt.

4. Swim to the surface.

* Once the car is partially filled with water, the pressure inside will equalize with the pressure outside, and you'll be able to open the door.

Adjust speed.

Push in the clutch.

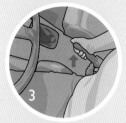

Engage the handbrake
as you . . .

. . . turn the wheel left from
twelve to six o'clock.

Snap back to twelve o'clock.

Release the handbrake.

Shift into first gear.

Accelerate.

Shift into first gear.

Let the clutch out.

Drive in a circle.

... while releasing
the handbrake.

Push in the clutch ...

Floor the accelerator ...

... while turning a
tight circle ...

... and pulling up the
handbrake.

127 ride the back wheel

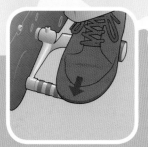
Shift into first gear.

Rev to two-thirds capacity.

Pull in the clutch; rev fully.

Sit back in the saddle.

128 do a smoky burnout

Use a car with bad tires.

Make a puddle of motor oil.

Get in; put on seat belt.

Drive over oil to coat tires.

Gas it; let out the clutch.

Cover rear brake to be safe.

Pull up; keep wheel straight.

Ease off throttle to land.

Push brake with left foot.

Hold brake; tap gas to jump.

Floor gas, releasing brake.

Make a smoky getaway.

rampage in the roller derby

In the 1920s, audiences first thrilled to sexy dames skating tough in the roller derby. Gameplay is simple—two jammers race around the track for two minutes, while the other team's blockers try to stop them.

The jam starts with the pivots leading the pack.

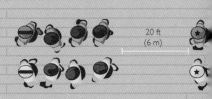

20 ft
(6 m)

The first through the pack is the jam's "lead jammer."

pivot
sets the pace,
serves as blocker

blocker
blocks opposing
team's jammer

jammer
passes as many
blockers as possible

Each player the jammer passes is worth one point.

Rough pushing, tripping, and brawling result in penalties.

Helmet markings declare your position in the pack.

Keep accessories minimal—less to grab onto!

Elbow and wrist guards are a must.

Sexy is good, but be sure your outfit lets you skate hard!

Wear those kneepads—you're going down.

Old-school boot skates give the stability you need.

The lead jammer ends a jam by placing hands on hips.

appreciate a power slam

Rally the crowd.

Stun with a kick to the solar plexus.

Toss opponent into ropes.

Grab him as he bounces back.

Use his momentum to swing him up.

Rotate; slam.

If possible, avoid conflict.

If not, try to appear insane.

Do something unexpected.

Grab a glass and a chair.

Scream at top volume.

shotgun a beer 74

Throw a drink at opponent.

Menace with the chair.

Run away.

Make a fist with thumb out.

Swing; draw in other arm.

Land with first two knuckles.

Assume a defensive stance.

Glue each tin square to
one arm of clothespin.

Tie a string between small
wood square and a tack.

Wire one tin piece to the
battery; rig other to buzzer.

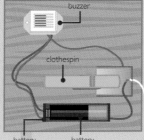

buzzer

clothespin

battery
holder

battery

Glue each component to
the large wood square.

Slide small wood square
between tin pieces.

Poke holes near edges
of small pieces.

Cut squares from balsa
wood and a pie tin.

Attach alarm to door; poke
tack into door frame.

To fool metal detectors, cut near an outlet.

Place valuables in the hole on the floor next to a stud.

Patch the drywall; repaint.

If you need to grab the goods quickly, kick in the wall.

136 shimmy up walls

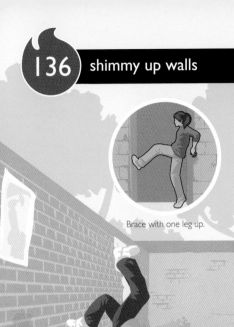

Brace with one leg up.

Bring up the other leg.

Lift with arms; walk up.

137 flip off a wall

Run; eye spot to plant foot.

Push off the ground.

Swing your left leg around.

Look at landing spot.

do a stuntman vault 138

Get a running start.

Plant your hand; jump.

Swing legs up and over.

Land with knees loose.

139 wrestle an alligator

Run in a zigzag pattern.

Can't flee? Press the neck.

Cover the eyes.

If bit, punch the snout.

140 fight a shark

Defend your back from the shark.

Hit on the side.

Pound the end of the nose.

Watch out in shallow water.

Take a deep breath; hold it.

Bite tail as hard as you can.

Grab a rock; strike head.

58 cook a meal in the dishwasher

Shove your hand in the gills.

Jab the shark in the eye.

Escape; treat any wounds immediately.

kyoketsu shoge
knife on cord

tessen
bladed fan

shuriken
throwing stars

neko-te
iron claws

kama
sickle

kakute
spiked ring

Drop two dinghies abaft.

Tie long rope to his hands.

Tie another rope to his feet.

Pilot dinghies to sides.

Drop prisoner in water.

Haul cur across barnacles.

Repeat as necessary.

Accept prisoner's apology.

Braid hemp; leave ends free.

Coat hemp ends in pitch.

Light the pitch on fire.

Attack.

145 pick your supervillain pet

Is a life of crime giving you high blood pressure? The simple act of menacingly petting a kitty reduces hypertension.

Highlight your tasteful, modern side with the clean lines and mechanical efficiency of sharks with lasers on their heads.

Nothing—nothing!—strikes fear into the hearts of men as effectively as an army of winged monkeys in bellhop outfits.

If you're an original gangster—an evil sorcerer, dark lord, or witch-king—kick it old school on an ancient fell beast.

146 stun with a poison dart

1 Boil the sap of the wourali vine with snake venom and magical herbs.

2 Dip a dart in the poison and load into your blowgun.

3 Fire!

54 fire rocket-powered spitballs

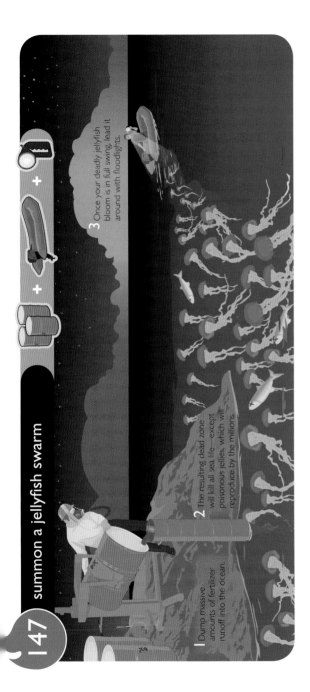

147 summon a jellyfish swarm

1 Dump massive amounts of fertilizer runoff into the ocean.

2 The resulting dead zone will kill all sea life—except poisonous jellies, which will reproduce by the millions.

3 Once your deadly jellyfish bloom is in full swing, lead it around with floodlights.

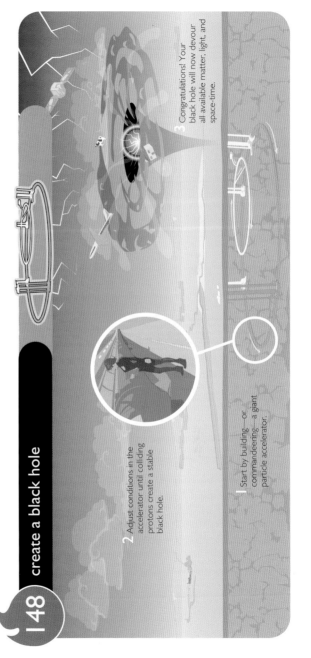

148 create a black hole

1 Start by building—or commandeering—a giant particle accelerator.

2 Adjust conditions in the accelerator until colliding protons create a stable black hole.

3 Congratulations! Your black hole will now devour all available matter, light, and space-time.

149 deflect a black hole

Spot oncoming black hole.

Fire H-bombs at it.

Hole is knocked off course.

HERO OF THE YEAR!

Limestone will react immediately with lava, releasing clouds of CO_2 and cooling the molten rock into a harmless solid.

150 avert a volcanic eruption

Detect impending eruption.

Erect giant limestone walls.

Drop limestone into lava.

Lava cools; villagers rejoice.

Identify deadly asteroid.

Pilot mass driver into space.

Land on asteroid.

Drill into asteroid's core.

Eject matter at high speed.

Return to Earth a hero.

The mass driver shoots rubble hard enough to alter the course of the asteroid, knocking it off a collision course with Earth. Hurray!

tools

 bucket

 can-can dress

 plain ammonia

 motorcycle

 jumpsuit

 absinthe

 aloe vera gel

 lighter

 hookah

 plastic jug

 electric toothbrush

 rhinestones

 fire extinguisher

 blowgun dart

 mp3 player

 spray bottle

 compost

 tobacco

 plastic bottle

 valve

 eyelash glue

 funnel

 space shuttle

 kiteboard

 alligator

 snake

 climbing rope

 cornstarch

 shortening

 flying suit

 clear tape

 heavy gloves

 kerosene

 sponge

 helicopter

 exfoliating pad

 tarp

 plaster of paris

 lovely assistant

 plate of food

 mechanical pencil

 earbuds

 seeds

 moss

 setting lotion

 stump remover

 chalk bag

 apple

 fabulous outfit

 polish applicator

 small spoons

 worali vine

 fuse

 car

 blue jeans

 rappel device

 magazine

 firework

electric guitar

 scissors

 plastic bottle

 jetpack suit

 dry ice

 dart

 craft glue

 fertilizer

 pushpin

 glass of wine

magical herbs

heavy books

motor oil

pipe

parachute

skydiving helmet

toolbox

scissors

ascot

cigarettes	dessert gelatin	barstool	kite	track bike	suitcases	nunchakus	paintbrush	torch
book	hard eyeliner	cake mix	bindle	rattail comb	blowgun	pirate ship	plank	ice cream
comic books	razor	pen	peaches	match	hammer	cardboard tube	balsa wood	fruit cocktail
train	gloves	alginate	pomade	torch	table	rope	craft stick	tack
straitjacket	pasties	pork tenderloin	travel stickers	cork	lawyer	rum	scotch	bread
hairpins	construction paper	pigs	oranges	red clay	fabric	moonshine	sandpaper	vegetable oil
ketchup	bowl	sugar	wire cutters	paddle brush	loot	tobacco	plywood	towel
jetpack	shaving brush	brown sugar	mini cereal boxes	dinghies	razor strop	cardboard	wig cap	shoe brush
makeup	small paintbrush	demerara sugar	varnish	paintbrush	chair	blender	shoe polish	tassels

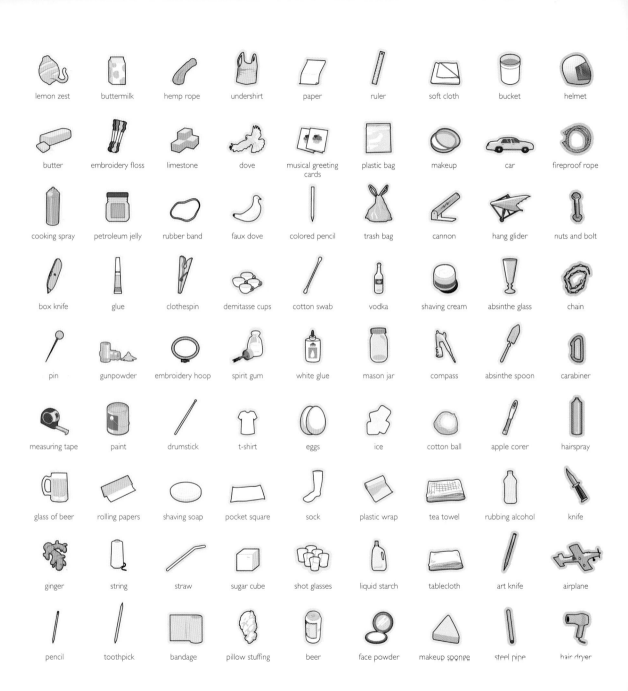

lemon zest	buttermilk	hemp rope	undershirt
paper	ruler	soft cloth	bucket	helmet

butter	embroidery floss	limestone	dove
musical greeting cards	plastic bag	makeup	car	fireproof rope

cooking spray	petroleum jelly	rubber band	faux dove
colored pencil	trash bag	cannon	hang glider	nuts and bolt

box knife	glue	clothespin	demitasse cups
cotton swab	vodka	shaving cream	absinthe glass	chain

pin	gunpowder	embroidery hoop	spirit gum
white glue	mason jar	compass	absinthe spoon	carabiner

measuring tape	paint	drumstick	t-shirt
eggs	ice	cotton ball	apple corer	hairspray

glass of beer	rolling papers	shaving soap	pocket square
sock	plastic wrap	tea towel	rubbing alcohol	knife

ginger	string	straw	sugar cube
shot glasses	liquid starch	tablecloth	art knife	airplane

pencil	toothpick	bandage	pillow stuffing
beer	face powder	makeup sponge	steel pipe	hair dryer

necklace	clamp	tweezers	comb	coffee grinder	pen	power drill	lipstick	speaker
plastic tubing	straight razor	screws	stepladder	seismograph	indelible pen	mascara	false eyelashes	thong
duct tape	strainer	embroidery needle	climbing shoes	glue gun	eyeliner	battery holder	strap lock	corset
pie tin	hairclips	keyhole saw	h-bombs	fireplace lighter	comb	makeup brush	charcoal	record
tongs	eyelash curler	shark	climbing harness	tankards	curling iron	battery	india ink	electrical tape
flask	beer keg	fireproof blanket	baking tin	kettle	jigsaw	pitch	shoe	coffee
saw	roller pan	strainer	rock	leaf blower	rotary tool	eyeshadow applicator	turntables	business suit
buzzer	staple gun	grater	massive drill	inflatable dinghy	screwdriver	jetpack helmet	heavy cream	full-coverage bra
enamel saucepan	hole saw drill bit	foil	mass driver	guitar string	nail	dartboard	waterproof lantern	

index

26

2

65

60

13

115 127 98 76 44

show me who

WELDON OWEN INC.

CEO, President Terry Newell

VP, Sales and
New Business Development Amy Kaneko

VP, Publisher Roger Shaw

Creative Director Kelly Booth

Executive Editor Mariah Bear

Editor Lucie Parker

Project Editor Frances Reade

Production Editor Emelie Griffin

Art Director Marisa Kwek

Senior Designer Stephanie Tang

Designers Delbarr Moradi, Meghan Hildebrand

Illustration Coordinators
Conor Buckley, Sheila Masson

Production Director Chris Hemesath

Production Manager Michelle Duggan

Production Coordinator Charles Mathews

Color Manager Teri Bell

weldon**owen**

415 Jackson Street, Suite 200
San Francisco, CA 94111
Telephone: 415 291 0100
Fax: 415 291 8841

www.wopublishing.com

Weldon Owen is a division of
BONNIER

Library of Congress data is on file with the Publisher.

ISBN: 978-1-61628-221-9

10 9 8 7 6 5 4 3 2

Printed in China by 1010 Printing Ltd.

Special thanks to:

Storyboarders
Sam Belletto, Alan Dap, Sarah Duncan, Kenneth Holland, Jonathan Shariat, Jamie Spinello, Brandi Valenza

Illustration specialists
Hayden Foell, Raymond Larrett, Jamie Spinello, Ross Sublett

Editorial and research support team
Ben Bracken, Lou Bustamante, Marc Caswell, Kat Engh, Michael Alexander Eros, Justin Goers, CJ Harris, Kevin Parks Hauser, Dave Jensen, Susan Jonaitis, Arrash Moradi, Ben Rosenberg, Mike Sheofsky, Marisa Solis

A **Show Me Now** Book.
Show Me Now is a trademark
of Weldon Owen Inc.
www.showmenow.com

ILLUSTRATION CREDITS The artwork in this book was a true team effort. We are happy to thank and acknowledge our illustrators.

Front Cover: Juan Calle (Liberum Donum): nunchakus Jessica Henry: guitar Vik Kulihin: motorcycle Stephanie Tang: turntable Otis Thomson: absinthe

Back Cover: Hayden Foell: blue blazer, cyclist Gabhor Utomo: straitjacket

Key bg=background, ex=extra art

Steve Baletsa: 35–37 Juan Calle (Liberum Donum): 1–2 bg, 6, 9 17–18, 39–40, 48–49, 101, 110, 113–114, 123, 129–133, 136–139, 141–144, 149–151 Sarah Duncan: 86, 92 Hayden Foell: 13, 46 bg, 68–69 Britt Hanson: 11–12, 55, 58, 80–81 bg, 82, 106 bg, 111–112 ex Jessica Henry: 34, 44 Pilar Erika Johnson: 38, 73–74 Vic Kulihin: 53–54, 67, 77, 99–100, 106–107, 125–128, 140 Raymond Larrett: 15–16, 57, 63–66, 73 ex, 76, 84, 108–109, 135 Christine Meighan: 7, 21–22, 25, 27, 59–60, 78, 118–120 Barbara Smullen: 46 Jamie Spinello: 85 Ross Sublett: 87 Bryon Thompson: 61–62, 70–72, 89, 96, 103 Otis Thomson: 14, 115 Taylor Tucek: 102 Gabhor Utomo: 3–5, 29–32, 41, 43, 45, 50–52, 56, 83, 88, 90–91, 104–105, 117, 118 bg, 121–122, 124, 145–148 Tina Cash Walsh: 8, 10, 19–20, 28, 33, 42, 79–81, 93–95 Mary Zins: 1–2, 23–24, 26, 47, 75, 98, 111–112, 116, 134

hey, you!

Yeah, you. Is there something awesome that you think should have been in this book? Do you have an amazing skill you want to share with the world? Is there something we didn't get quite right? If so, we want to know about it!

We love hearing from our highly talented readers. Send us your ideas, feedback, or even photos or video of you demonstrating your sweet skills (nothing pervy or dangerous, kids), and you could be featured in the next Show Me Now book.

We can't wait to hear from you!

 www.showmenow.com

 ATTN: SHOW ME TEAM
Weldon Owen Inc.
415 Jackson Street
San Francisco, California 94111